HARVEST FESTIVALS
Harvest

Lois Rock

LION
Children's Books

Introduction

Published by
Lion Publishing plc
Sandy Lane West, Oxford, England
www.lion-publishing.co.uk
ISBN 0 7459 3908 2

First edition 1999
10 9 8 7 6 5 4 3 2 1 0

Typeset in 18/21 Baskerville MT Schoolbook
Printed and bound in Singapore

Acknowledgments
'We Plough the Fields and Scatter' (spread 1): tune by
J.A.P. Schultz; words by Matthias Claudius (1740–1815),
translated by Jane Campbell (1817–78).
'Come, Ye Thankful people, Come' (spread 20): tune by
George Elvey (1816–93); words by Henry Alford (1810–71).

This book is one of a series dealing with the Christian festivals.

This one is about the joyful season of harvest.

Here are recipes that celebrate the harvest and a variety of craft items, including all you need to organize a harvest meal to share with others.

Here, too, are traditional hymns and songs and prayers of thanksgiving.

Here is a book to deepen a child's understanding of the Christian heritage.

Contents

1 Harvest Magic

Every year, people sow seeds. When the weather is right, the seeds sprout. They grow into plants, with roots and shoots, leaves and flowers, fruits and seeds. From these, people—and animals—have a harvest of food to enjoy. How does this magic happen?

Pepper

Those who believe in a God who made the world give thanks to that Great Maker.

In Christian churches, there is often a celebration— a harvest festival.

Carrot

Onion

People say thank you to God, and they also meet together to share food at a harvest supper. They often prepare gifts of food to share with others, believing that the God who gives the harvest wants all people in the world to have enough to eat.

Lettuce

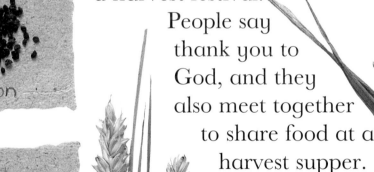

Radish

Tomato

Bean

We Plough the Fields and Scatter

Here is a Christian hymn of thanks for the harvest. In the hymn, God is also called 'the Lord'.

Treble Recorder
Guitar tacet

We plough the fields, and scat-ter the good seed on the

F C G C F G Am Dm G

land, but it is fed and wat-ered by God's al-migh-ty

C F/C C7 F C7 F

hand; He sends the snow in win-ter, the warmth to swell the

C Guitar tacet C F

grain, the breez-es and the sun-shine, And soft re-fresh-ing rain:

Refrain

F C F C F C

All good gifts a-round us are sent from heaven a-bove, then

F C F C Dm A Dm F Gm F/C C F

thank the Lord, O thank the Lord, for all _____ his love.

2 Weather Watch

People who sow seeds watch the weather every day. The seeds need rain: in the moist soil, they will swell and sprout. The seeds need sun: the root will grow down into the warm soil; the shoot will grow up towards the light. In the sun, the leaves will unfold, and the plant will grow.

Here's how to keep a chart of the weather. Here are pictures for a sunny day, a cloudy day, a day with cloud and sun, a rainy day and a thunderstorm.

Weather chart

You will need

paper, torn or cut into squares

crayons or pastels

1 Work out simple pictures for each type of weather.

2 Draw a picture on a square of paper every day, and display them in order.

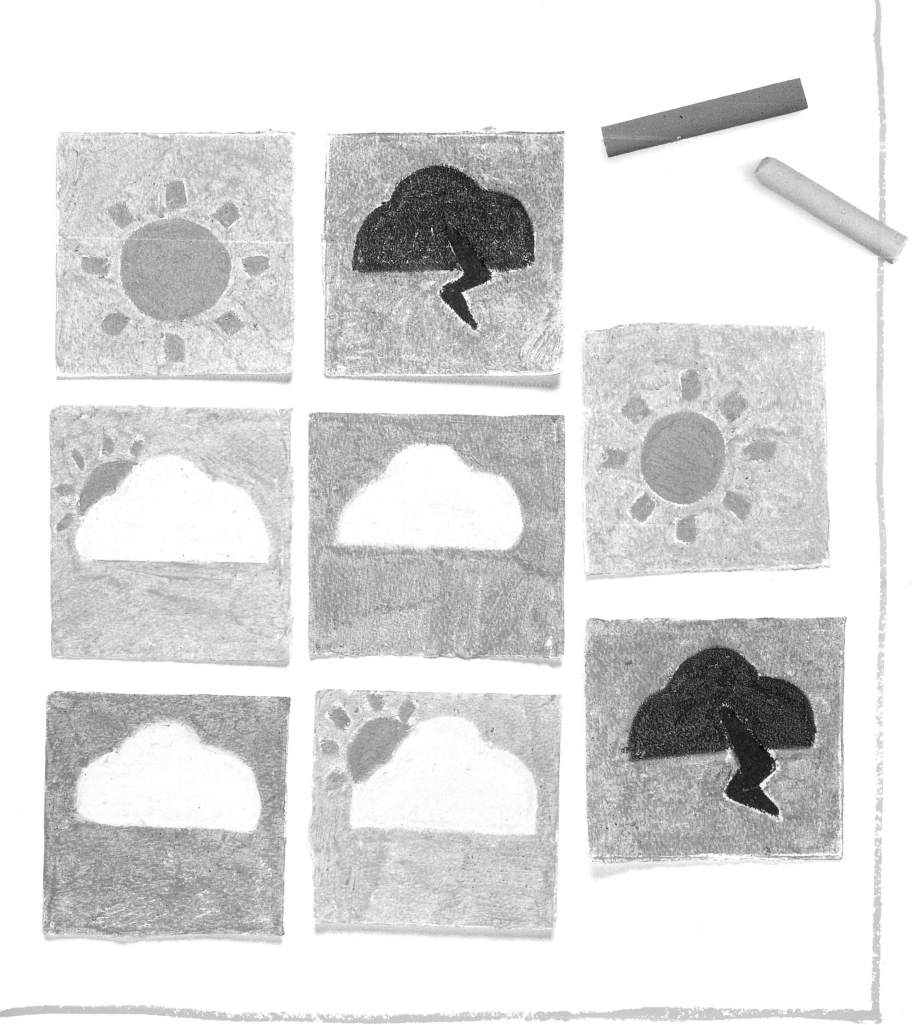

3 Quick Crops

Seeds take a little while to grow. When you sow seeds in the ground, the soil seems to stay bare for days. Be patient. As long as the seeds are kept in moist soil and in a place as warm as a spring day, the seeds will grow.

Think of all the types of leaves people grow to eat!

Lettuce crop

You will need

flowerpot

soil

lettuce seeds

watering-can

1 Fill a flowerpot with soil. Press it gently to firm it. Sprinkle just a tiny pinch of lettuce seeds on top.

2 Sprinkle a handful of soil on top. Water gently.

3 Wait for the lettuces to grow. As they do, nip off some seedlings to leave just one lettuce plant growing in its own space.

mint

coriander

spinach

parsley

another type of lettuce

some lettuces have reddish leaves

basil

this lettuce has really curly leaves

4 Flowers

When seeds grow, they send out a root and a shoot, and the seed leaves unfold. The stem grows longer, and the real leaves begin to grow. After a while, flower buds appear, and then the full blooms.

Bees, butterflies and other insects travel from flower to flower, sipping the sweet nectar in the flower. As they travel, they pick up a dust called pollen, and some of it brushes off onto the next flower. This pollen is needed to make the seeds grow behind the flower. Slowly, the flower fades, and the seed head swells.

Lavender bags

You will need

lavender in flower

plate

silk, cut into 15 cm squares

ribbon

Sometimes flowers are harvested because they smell so sweet. Make lavender gifts from a harvest of lavender.

1 Pick stems of lavender flowers and dry them: either hang them in a cool, dry place for four weeks, or microwave them on the lowest setting for 30 minutes! Strip the flower heads onto a plate.

2 Take a square of silk and put a heap of flower heads in the middle. Fold up the lower point as shown.

3 Fold in the sides, taking care that the point of the second side just reaches to the edge.

4 Turn the parcel round and fold the remaining point up to meet the opposite folded edge. Take care that the point reaches just to the edge.

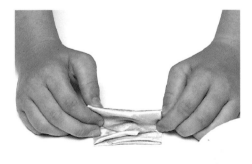

5 Fold the whole parcel in half again so the edges just meet.

6 Tie a bow round the middle of your silk parcel. The lavender bag can be put in any cupboard of clothes, and you will smell the lavender each time you open the cupboard for many weeks.

5 Seeds and Fruits

Some of the crops people eat are seeds.

French beans are a bit like slim runner beans. People usually eat the pods whole.

Pea plants have pods with fat, green seeds inside.

Runner bean flowers are red. When the petals fall, you can see a tiny seed pod just beginning to grow. In just a couple of weeks, the pods grow long, like the ones here. It takes a couple of weeks more for the seeds to grow large. However, people mostly eat runner beans when the seeds are still small.

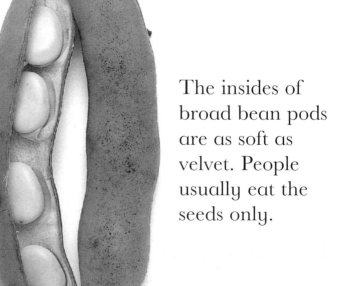

The insides of broad bean pods are as soft as velvet. People usually eat the seeds only.

Other plants have fat, juicy fruits in which the seeds are kept safe. People often eat the juicy tomato fruit whole, the flesh and the seeds together.

Pepper fruits have a cluster of white seeds inside. People cut the seeds away and eat the sweet skin.

Look at the seeds growing inside this crisp, pale cucumber. People eat the fruit together with the young seeds.

6 Roots

Some crops are the part of the plant that grow underground. They are usually called roots.

Radishes are a quick-to-grow root crop. They have a very tangy taste.

Onions grow underground. Their juicy layers are really underground leaves.

Carrots are roots.

One Potato, Two Potato

Chorus More Lively

Verse 2:

I'm going to grow so many things,
I'll surely never starve,
Cabbages and cauliflowers
I won't do things by half.
I'll plant a row of runner beans,
They'll grow so very high.
With a bit of sun and a bit of rain
They'll reach up to the sky—oh! *(Chorus)*

Potatoes develop underground. They are a type of tuber—they grow out from the roots.

7 Harvest Soup

This soup uses different types of crops: leaves of lettuce and mint, seeds from pea pods, onion roots and the underground tubers of the potato plant!

You will need

1 onion

1 potato

50 g butter

500 ml water

1 head of lettuce

3–4 sprigs of mint

300 g peas

milk or cream

salt and pepper

chopping board and sharp knife

large pan

wooden spoon

blender (for a grown-up to use)

☺ *Ask a grown-up to help you cook.*

☺ *Always wash your hands before you begin.*

In this recipe, it is a good idea for your grown-up helper to do any stirring while the pan is on the heat and to lift the pan down onto a heatproof worksurface for you to add extra ingredients and so on.

1 Ask a grown-up to help you peel the onion and the potato, using a sharp knife. Cut each in half.

2 Chop each half: first make three slices lengthways. Then hold the slices together and chop in the other direction.

3 Ask a grown-up to melt the butter in a large pan. Lift the pan onto the work-surface and add the chopped potato and onion.

4 Stir gently until the vegetables are shiny and just turning pale gold. Add the water. Then ask a grown-up to put the pan back on the heat to simmer for about 15 minutes.

5 While you wait, tear up the lettuce. Rinse the leaves in cold water to remove any dirt or dust. Pull the mint leaves off the stems and get the peas ready.

6 Have the pan lifted onto the worksurface and add the lettuce and peas. Have the pan put back on the heat and let it simmer for about 10 minutes. Turn off the heat.

7 Ask a grown-up to lift the pan onto the worksurface and to make the mixture smooth using a blender.

8 Then add a little milk or cream to make the soup as runny as you like it. Stir together and add a little salt and pepper. Heat gently, and then serve in bowls.

8 Harvest Loaf

Say the word 'harvest' and many people think of a field of grain, turning gold as it ripens in the sun.

A lot of the bread we eat is made from a grain called wheat. The seeds ripen in a cluster at the top of a stalk. This cluster is called an ear. Each grain seed is covered in a papery husk.

To harvest the grain, the husk is rubbed off the seed and blown away. The seed is then taken away to be ground up to a powder: flour. The flour is made into bread.

First the seed
And then the grain;
Thank you, God,
For sun and rain.
First the flour
And then the bread;
Thank you, God,
That we are fed.

Blow, wind, blow!
And go, mill, go!
That the miller may grind his corn;
That the baker may take it,
And into bread make it,
And bring us a loaf in the morn.

Harvest bread

You will need

750 g flour

1 tbsp salt

1 packet yeast

1 tbsp oil

450 ml water

bowl

spoon

extra flour

scissors

baking parchment

baking tray

blunt knife

wire rack

clean earthenware flowerpots

1 Put the flour, salt, yeast and oil into a bowl. Add a little water and stir. Do this till the mixture forms lumps. With clean hands, gather the mix into one lump. Add extra water if you need to. This is the 'dough'.

2 Sprinkle some extra flour onto a clean worksurface and lift the dough onto it. Squeeze and push it with your hands for about 10 minutes, till it is smooth and shiny.

3 Cut a square of baking parchment big enough to line each flowerpot. Push it in. Don't worry about the bits that stick up above.

4 Take lumps of dough big enough to fill each pot a little more than half full. Shape them into sausage shapes and smooth them in.

5 Put the pots on a baking tray and leave the loaves to rise till the dough is just showing over the rim. Put them in the oven to bake for about 15 minutes.

6 Ask a grown-up to help decide if the loaves are done. The tops should be slightly brown and hard to the touch. Take them out of the oven. Leave for 5 minutes. Then unwrap them and put them on a rack to finish cooling.

9 Harvest Meadow

Harvest is not just for people—all the animals need food as well! Through the summer, cows can graze on meadow plants. Some meadows are allowed to grow long. Then they are cut and the plants dry in the sun. This dry hay is collected into barns, to be food for the animals through the winter.

The cows provide milk that people can drink. Milk can also be used to make cheese and butter.

Here's how to make some butter to eat with your bread.

Butter

You will need

double cream

2 bowls

whisk

sieve

jug of water

1 Put the cream in a bowl. Whisk it until it is stiff.

2 Keep whisking in short 'whizzes' until the cream begins to separate into yellow bits in pale milk. Keep giving shorter 'whizzes' until these form bigger lumps.

3 Put the sieve over the second bowl and tip the mix in. The thin milk will go through, leaving lumps of butter. (You can use the thin 'buttermilk' to drink, or to make something—such as the harvest soup!)

4 Hold the sieve of butter over the first bowl and pour water over it to wash it very gently. Leave to drain.

☺ *Ask a grown-up to help you cook.*

☺ *Always wash your hands before you begin.*

10 Harvest Fruits

Some crops are ready to harvest just a few months after they are planted as seeds.

Others grow on bushes or trees that do not bear fruit until they are several years old. Then they may give good fruits year after year.

Rosy Apple

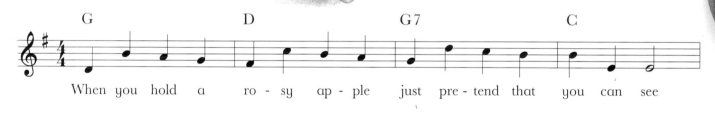

When you hold a ro-sy ap-ple just pre-tend that you can see

through its walls so round and shi-ny to a sleep-ing fa — mi-ly.

Moth-er seed and her brown ba-bies cud-dled up so co-si-ly

and they dream that some-day may-be each will be an ap-ple tree.

The Johnny Appleseed grace

There is a tale that, long ago in America, a man went round sowing appleseeds wherever he could. The seeds grew into trees, and produced much fruit. People were grateful for the good harvests they were able to enjoy.

Johnny Appleseed

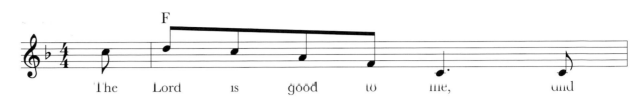

The Lord is good to me, and

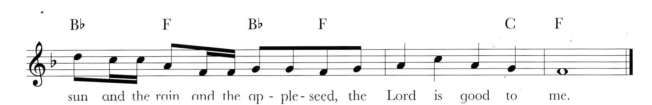

so I thank the Lord, for giv - ing me the things I need, the

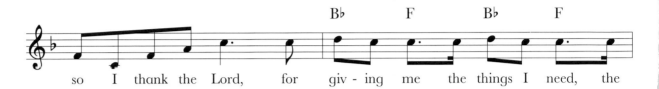

sun and the rain and the ap - ple - seed, the Lord is good to me.

11 Harvest Crumble

Think of the different crops used in this dessert: there is flour, which is ground from seeds of wheat; sugar which is made in a factory from the sweetness in a root crop called sugar beet; butter, made from the milk of cows who munch on meadow grasses; and two types of fruit— apples and blackberries.

Blackberry and apple crumble

You will need

3 or 4 large cooking apples

4 tbsp water

100 g blackberries, washed

2–3 tbsp sugar

150 g flour

100 g sugar

100 g butter

apple peeler

chopping board

sharp knife

large saucepan

wooden spoon

baking dish

bowl

oven mitts

☺ Ask a grown-up to help you cook. Have them preheat the oven to 200°C.

☺ Wash your hands before you begin.

To make the crumble

To prepare the fruit

I Put the flour and sugar into the bowl.

1 Carefully peel your apples using an apple peeler.

2 Put the apples on the chopping board. Hold one apple firmly and carefully chop chunks away by cutting down with the knife. Repeat with the other apples.

2 Add the butter and, using your fingertips, break it into tiny pieces in the flour and sugar mix. Soon the mix will look a bit like breadcrumbs.

3 Put the apple chunks in a pan with the water. Cook over a gentle heat for about 15 minutes until the apple goes soft and fluffy. Stir the apples every few minutes so nothing sticks to the bottom of the pan.

4 Lift the pan off the heat and add the blackberries and sugar. Turn the mixture into the baking dish and smooth it with the wooden spoon.

3 Tip the crumble mix over the fruit and smooth it off. Bake in the oven for 20 minutes. Ask a grown-up to help lift it out. Serve hot, warm—or cold!

12 Harvest Supper

When the harvest is good, people can be thankful that there will be food to buy in the months ahead.

One traditional way of celebrating good harvests is to have a feast, and share it with lots of people.

Whom will you invite to a harvest supper?

1 Mark a rectangle of thin card 120 mm x 360 mm and cut it out using a craft knife against a ruler on a cutting mat.

2 Measure the 120 mm and 240 mm points along both long edges. Line a ruler up against each pair and fold the card up along the edge. Refold the card along the fold lines so it forms a Z.

Invitation cards

You will need

pencil and ruler

thin card

cutting board and craft knife

scissors

thicker card

coloured paper

white paper to print on

scrap paper

leaves in different shapes

paints and brushes

glue

writing pen

6 Carefully lift the leaf up by the stalk and lay it paint side up on the other pad of scrap paper. Take a piece of the paper you want to print on and lay it carefully on top of the leaf.

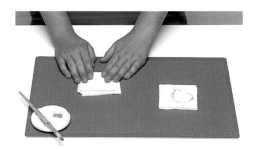

7 Rub your finger carefully over the paper, taking care not to move it.

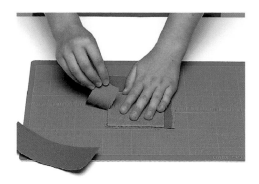

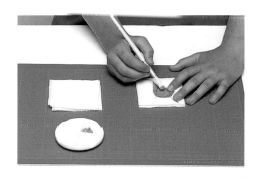

3 Cut a square of thick card 100 mm x 100 mm. Lay it on a piece of background paper and hold it down while you tear the background paper to the same shape. Glue onto the front of the card.

4 Cut squares of white paper 80 mm x 80 mm. Cut three pieces for each card.

5 Begin printing. Have two piles of scrap paper ready. Put a leaf, ridged side up, on one pile and paint all over it, right to the edges.

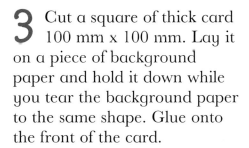

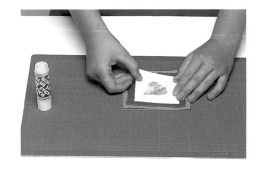

8 Peel the printed paper away from the leaf and leave it to dry. Throw away the top piece of scrap paper from each pile so you start each print with a fresh piece. Make one print only for each card.

9 When the prints are dry, glue a print onto the front of each card.

10 Open the Z-shaped card and glue a plain piece of card on each of the two panels showing. When the glue is dry, write your invitation on the plain pieces.

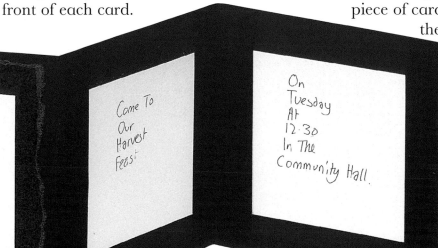

Come To
Our
Harvest
Feast

On
Tuesday
At
12.30
In The
Community Hall.

13 Harvest Placemats

Make placemats and napkin-rings for your harvest supper table.

Place settings

You will need

scissors

a piece of thick card cut to 350 mm x 250 mm

ruler and pencil

paper in different colours

masking tape

glue

To make the mats

1 Take your rectangle of thick card. Mark a grid of squares on the card, each 50 mm apart.

2 For each mat, begin by placing the thick card onto a sheet of coloured paper. Press on the card and tear the paper to the same shape by pulling upwards along one edge of the card. Do the same for all the edges. Now tear another rectangle in a contrasting colour.

3 Lay the card on one sheet of paper with one square of the grid jutting beyond the edge on one side and 50 mm of the paper showing at the other side. Tear the paper along the card, almost to the lower edge. Move the card one square over and repeat. Do this all the way across. Tear the other colour paper in the opposite direction.

4 Now line up the two torn rectangles so you can tear off a strip at a time from one and weave it into the other. When you have used all of the strips, adjust them so they fit together well.

To make napkin-rings

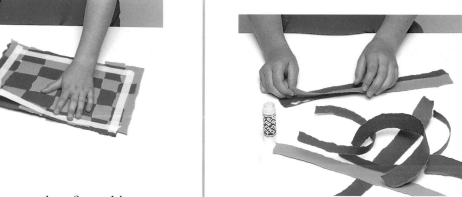

5 Place a strip of masking tape to hold the strips in place, as shown in the photograph. Turn the placemat over.

1 To make napkin-rings, take two strips of paper, each about 18 cm long. Glue them so one overlaps the other.

2 Curl into a circle and fasten on the inside.

Make everyone welcome at the table. At a harvest meal in the Christian community, prayers of thanks to God are said. Here are two:

The bread is warm and fresh,
The water cool and clear.
Lord of all life, be with us,
Lord of all life, be near.

God is great,
God is good,
Thank you, God,
For all our food.

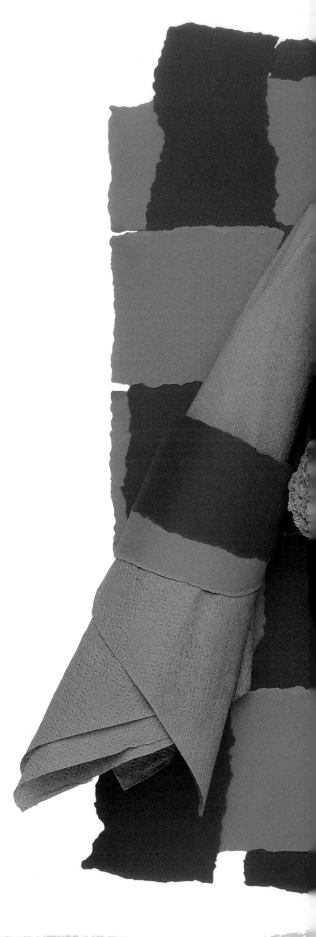

15 Harvest Store

At harvest time, there is plenty of food. There may be too much of some crops to eat at once!

Some crops, such as the flour from wheat, do not go bad as long as they are kept cool and dry. Others need to be preserved. Making jam is one way of preserving the luscious fruits of summer.

Raspberry jam

You will need

450 g raspberries

450 g granulated sugar

colander

large saucepan

wooden spoon

small plate

2 or 3 jamjars

2 wooden boards

small jug

wax discs

clear jamjar covers

oven mitts

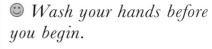

☺ *Wash your hands before you begin.*

☺ *A grown-up should be in charge of the saucepan and of turning the heat up and down. Also, ask a grown-up to get the jars really clean: they must be washed carefully in hot water, then left to dry in an oven set at 100°C.*

1 Wash the raspberries in the colander and let them drain. Put the washed fruit in the pan. Heat it gently till juice flows out. Then turn up the heat and let it boil.

2 Ask a grown-up to help lift the pan off the heat and add the sugar. Stir with the wooden spoon till the sugar dissolves. Put the pan back on the heat and let it boil for 5 minutes.

3 Lift the pan off the heat onto a wooden board. Put a spoonful of the jam mixture on the plate and leave it to cool for a minute. Touch it gently. If you see the surface crinkle, the jam is ready. If not, boil it for 2 minutes more and try again.

4 Put the jamjars on the other wooden board. Dip the jug into the jam and pour it, a little at a time, into the jars.

5 Put a wax disc on the top of the hot jam. Let it cool, then add a clear cover. Add a pretty cover on top and label your jam (see spread 16).

16 Harvest Gifts

How good it is if people who have food share it with others! Here is a way to turn your harvest jams into pretty gifts.

Pretty jamjar covers

You will need

small plate

coloured paper

pencil

ruler

scissors

rubber bands

raffia

writing pen

glue

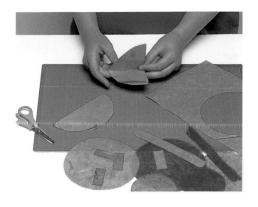

1 Draw round a plate on the coloured paper. The circle should be a little bigger than the clear jamjar cover. With a ruler and pencil, draw a label-sized rectangle. Cut these two shapes out with scissors.

2 Fold the circle in half, in half again and in half again.

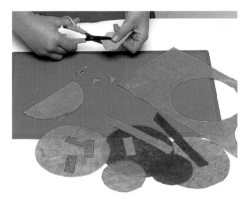

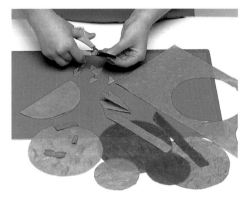

3 Snip round the edges to create a lacy pattern, as shown in the photograph.

4 Fold the rectangle in half and in half again and snip the edges of that.

5 Unfold the cover and centre it on the jamjar. Hold it in place with a rubber band, and cover it with raffia. Write the type of jam on the label. Glue it onto the jamjar.

17 Harvest Box

Giving gifts of food is an important harvest tradition.

In many places, people first bring gifts of food to church. There is a service of thanksgiving—of thanking God, who Christians believe sends the harvest. The food gifts are then given away. Sometimes, the gift is most important because the person really needs food. At other times, the gift is important because it is a way of saying that the person is loved and remembered.

Make a harvest box and fill it with good things to give!

You will need

a piece of corrugated cardboard 420 mm x 280 mm

ruler and pencil

small plate

cutting board

craft knife

skewer

raffia

thick, blunt needle

1 Mark lines on your card, as shown in the photograph at the end of the book. Then, using a small plate, draw a curve at each end. Shade in the parts to be cut away. Cut out, using a cutting board and craft knife.

2 Mark the fold lines by drawing round the centre square and the tabs with a pencil, pressing hard as you do so, to crease the card.

3 Fold the card up, using the ruler held against the fold line to keep the crease straight.

4 Fold the box into place with the tabs inside the ends. As you hold the card, ask a grown-up to punch holes with a skewer through the ends at the points shown in the photograph, going through both thicknesses.

5 Thread the needle with several strands of raffia. Working on one side, take the raffia through a hole from the outside in, then back to the outside again through the other hole in that same side, as shown. Pull the ends to the same length and tie in a knot. Do the same on the other side.

18 The Animals' Harvest

The harvest is not just for people. Roots and shoots, leaves and stems, flowers, fruit and seeds provide food for many animals and birds. In this country, where there is enough food for all, it is possible to use foodstuffs for crafts you can't eat!

Make a harvest display with these claydough mice and birds!

☺ *Ask a grown-up to preheat the oven to 100°C.*

Dough creatures

You will need

200 g plain white flour

100 g salt

cold water

mixing bowl

wooden spoon

pencil

baking tray

baking parchment

wire rack

paint and paintbrush

clear glaze and paintbrush

I Put the flour and salt in the bowl. Add the water slowly and stir and knead until you have a dough that will hold its shape.

2 Take small balls of dough and shape them into mice or birds. Shape the mouse ears and tail separately, and 'glue' them with a little cold water.

3 Line the baking tray with parchment and put the birds and animals on them. Mark the eye holes with a pencil point. Use the blunt end of the pencil to mark 'feathers' on the bird. Bake overnight. Then turn off the oven and let it cool for a while. Lift the animals out onto a wire rack. Leave them out to dry for a couple of days more.

To make your birds and mice look really attractive, paint them gold. When the paint is dry, brush on a clear glaze.

19 Harvest Game

You have been picking apples in the orchard. Make your way across the fields to Home Farm.

When you have played this game, you can try making your own game board with as many fields as you choose!

To play

playing pieces

a die

1. Players put their pieces in the apple orchard at the start.

2. Take it in turns to throw the die. If you throw the number of a type of field next to the one you're in (see key at the top of the opposite page), you can move into it.

3. If you do not throw the number of a field next to you, you must stay where you are.

4. You can move over a bridge in one go, if you throw the number matching the field on the other side.

5. The winner is the player who reaches Home Farm first. Throw a six to get you there from a next-door field.

1

2

3

4

5

6

HOME FARM

20 Harvest Home

Gather together some of the foods you eat each day. Think of the crops that have been harvested so that you can be fed. Think of all the people who work to bring you the things you need.

Think of all the reasons you have to give thanks.

Come, Ye Thankful People, Come

Come, ye thank-ful peo-ple, come, raise the song of har-vest-home!

All be safe-ly gath-ered in, ere the win-ter storms be-gin;

God, our Mak-er, doth pro-vide for our wants to be sup-plied;

Come to God's own tem-ple, come; Raise the song of har-vest-home!

Mark the corrugated cardboard as follows to make your harvest box (see spread 17). Remember these shapes are only a guide and should not be copied exactly. Follow the measurements shown.